READING POWER

Westward Ho!

THE GOLD RUSH

CALIFORNIA OR BUST!

EMILY RAABE

The Rosen Publishing Group's
PowerKids Press™
New York

Published in 2003 by The Rosen Publishing Group, Inc.
29 East 21st Street, New York, NY 10010

Copyright © 2003 by The Rosen Publishing Group, Inc.

First Edition

Book Design: Michael DeLisio

Photo Credits: Cover, pp. 9, 14–15, 16, 18–19 © Hulton/Archive/Getty Images; pp. 4, 8 Michael DeLisio; pp. 5, 6–7, 12–13 North Wind Picture Archives; pp. 10, 11 Library of Congress Geography and Map Division; p. 17 © AP/Wide World Photos; pp. 20–21 © Dave Bartruff/Corbis

Library of Congress Cataloging-in-Publication Data

Raabe, Emily.
The gold rush : California or bust! / Emily Raabe.
    p. cm. — (Westward ho!)
Summary: Describes how the 1848 discovery of gold at Sutter's Mill, California, sparked a movement of people to California from around the country and the world.
Includes bibliographical references and index.
ISBN 0-8239-6494-9 (lib. bdg.)
1. California—Gold discoveries—Juvenile literature. 2. Pioneers—California—History—19th century—Juvenile literature. 3. Frontier and pioneer life—California—Juvenile literature. [1. Gold mines and mining. 2. California—History—1846-1850. 3. Frontier and pioneer life—California.] I. Title.
F865 .R23 2003
979.4'04—dc21

                                    2002000504

Contents

Gold in the Hills   4

Getting to the Gold   6

Looking for Gold   12

Coming to America
    for Gold   19

After the Gold Rush   20

Glossary   22

Resources   23

Index/Word Count   24

Note   24

GOLD IN THE HILLS

On January 24, 1848, James Marshall discovered gold in a stream at Sutter's Mill in California. John Sutter owned the sawmill. Marshall and Sutter tried to keep the news a secret. However, people soon heard about the gold they found. The California Gold Rush was about to begin.

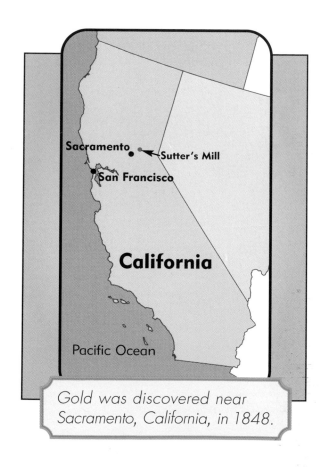

Gold was discovered near Sacramento, California, in 1848.

James Marshall

GETTING TO THE GOLD

People from all over the country went to California to find gold. They wanted to become rich. Most people traveled west in wagons pulled by oxen or horses. Some trips took as long as six months. Supplies of food and water often ran low. Many people died from hunger or thirst during their long trips.

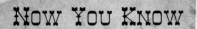

Now You Know

Wagons had to cross the mountains to get to California. People could die if they got trapped in the mountains during a snowstorm.

Settlers often walked alongside their wagons. They could travel about two miles an hour. The trip was about 2,000 miles.

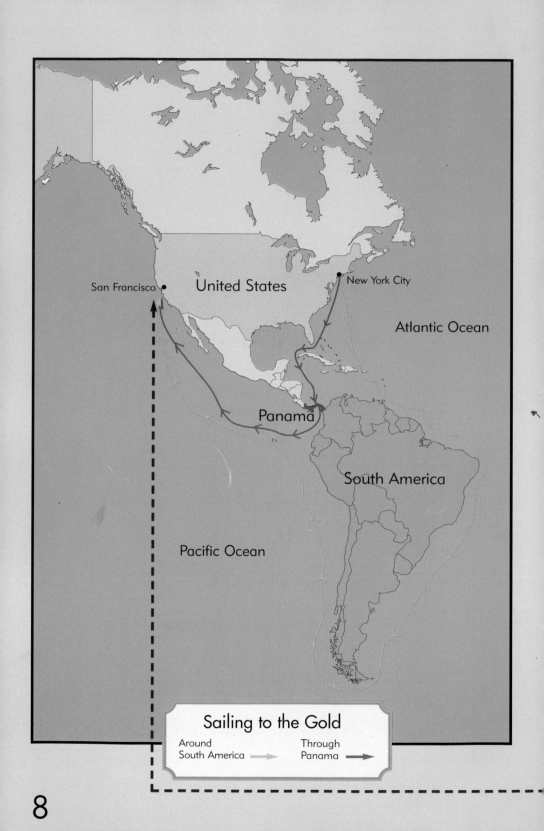

San Francisco

United States

New York City

Atlantic Ocean

Panama

South America

Pacific Ocean

Sailing to the Gold

Around
South America ➡️

Through
Panama ➡️

Many people on the East Coast sailed to California. There were two ways to get there by boat. One way was to sail to Panama and travel through the jungle to get to the Pacific Ocean. Then the people would have to find a boat to take them to California. Another way to reach California was to sail around the tip of South America.

Travelers often waited months to get a ship from Panama to San Francisco. Many prospectors would camp on the beaches while waiting for a ship.

In 1848, only 15,000 people lived in California.

BEFORE THE GOLD RUSH

San Francisco was once a small town with few homes or businesses.

By the end of 1849, there were almost 100,000 people living there.

AFTER THE GOLD RUSH

After 1848, San Francisco grew quickly because many people looking for gold settled there.

Looking for Gold

Most prospectors who came to California looked for gold in streams. They stood in ice-cold water up to their knees. They picked up sand and gravel from the bottom of the stream with a flat dish called a pan.

People who look for gold are called prospectors.

When prospectors shook their pans, water splashed out of the side, washing out the sand. Then the prospectors searched the gravel left in the pans for bits of gold.

Prospectors worked as many as ten hours a day in the hot California sun. Living conditions in their camps were very poor. However, because gold was so valuable, prospectors were willing to work hard. They struggled to find even a single flake of gold. Many prospectors gave up and left.

The people who came to California looking for gold were called forty-niners. This was because many of them came to California in 1849.

Not everyone went to California to look for gold. Many people went to set up businesses that sold supplies to prospectors. One man, Levi Strauss, started a company that made very strong pants for the prospectors. The company soon became the largest maker of denim pants, or jeans.

After gold was weighed, it could be used like money and be traded for goods in a store.

Five and a half nickels weigh as much as 1 ounce of gold.

Levi Strauss became wealthy without ever having to look for gold.

People from different countries worked side by side as they tried to find gold.

18

Coming to America for Gold

People also came from Europe, Asia, and South America to look for gold in California. People from more than 70 countries joined in the gold rush. After the gold rush ended, many of these people stayed to live in western cities, such as San Francisco and Sacramento.

AFTER THE GOLD RUSH

By 1853, about 250,000 people had gone to the California goldfields. As gold became harder to find, the California Gold Rush came to an end. The gold rush only lasted for about five years. However, it was the biggest reason for the early growth of California.

Many prospectors in the California Gold Rush barely found enough gold to pay for their supplies and their trip west.

Glossary

California Gold Rush (kal-uh-**for**-nyuh **gohld ruhsh**) a time beginning in 1848 when people from all over the world came to California to look for gold in the streams and soil

denim (**dehn**-uhm) a strong cloth made out of cotton that is used to make jeans

gravel (**grav**-uhl) small round pieces of rock

jungle (**juhng**-guhl) a thick forest of trees, bushes, and vines

oxen (**ahk**-suhn) animals that are like cows and are often used to pull things

prospectors (**prahs**-pehk-tuhrz) people who look for gold or other things of value

route (**root**) a path taken to get somewhere

valuable (**val**-yoo-uh-bul) worth a lot of money

wealthy (**wehl**-thee) owning a lot of money or land

Resources

Books

Dame Shirley and the Gold Rush
by James J. Rawls
Raintree Steck-Vaughn (1993)

Gold Fever! Tales from the California Gold Rush
by Rosalyn Schanzer (editor)
National Geographic Society (1999)

Web Sites

Due to the changing nature of Internet links, PowerKids
Press has developed an on-line list of Web sites related
to the subjects of this book. This site is updated regularly.
Please use this link to access the list:

http://www.powerkidslinks.com/wh/gold/

Index

C
California Gold Rush,
    4, 20–21
camps, 14

D
denim, 16

G
gravel, 12–13

J
jungle, 9

M
Marshall, James, 4–5

O
oxen, 6

P
Panama, 8–9
prospectors, 12–14,
    16, 21

S
Sacramento, 4, 19
San Francisco, 4,
    8–11, 19
Strauss, Levi, 16–17
Sutter, John, 4
Sutter's Mill, 4

Word Count: 469

Note to Librarians, Teachers, and Parents

If reading is a challenge, Reading Power is a solution! Reading Power is perfect for readers who want high-interest subject matter at an accessible reading level. These fact-filled, photo-illustrated books are designed for readers who want straightforward vocabulary, engaging topics, and a manageable reading experience. With clear picture/text correspondence, leveled Reading Power books put the reader in charge. Now readers have the power to get the information they want and the skills they need in a user-friendly format.